AMAZING
ORiGAMi

SEA MONSTERS AND FLYING MONSTERS

Gareth Stevens
PUBLISHING

Joe Fullman

Please visit our website, **www.garethstevens.com**.
For a free color catalog of all our high-quality books,
call toll free 1-800-542-2595 or fax 1-877-542-2596.

Cataloging-in-Publication Data
Names: Pullman, Joe.
Title: Sea monsters and flying monsters / Joe Pullman.
Description: New York : Gareth Stevens Publishing, 2019. | Series: Amazing origami | Includes glossary and index.
Identifiers: ISBN 9781538234686 (pbk.) | ISBN 9781538234709 (library bound) | ISBN 9781538234693 (6pack)
Subjects: LCSH: Origami--Juvenile literature. | Sea monsters in art--Juvenile literature. | Monsters in art--Juvenile literature.
Classification: LCC TT872.5 F85 2019 | DDC 736'.982--dc23

First Edition

Published in 2019 by
Gareth Stevens Publishing
111 East 14th Street, Suite 349
New York, NY 10003

Copyright © Arcturus Holdings Ltd, 2019

Models created by Picnic
Photography by Michael Wilkes
Text by Joe Fullman
Design by Emma Randall

Printed in the United States of America

CPSIA compliance information: Batch #CW19GS: For further information contact Gareth Stevens, New York, New York at 1-800-542-2595.

CONTENTS

INTRODUCTION

Get ready to explore the world of dinosaur-era origami. You'll learn how to make amazing flying and swimming reptiles, from a snapping Spinosaurus to a terrifying Pteranodon.

A lot of the origami models in this book are made with the same folds and basic designs, known as "bases." This introduction explains some of the ones that will appear most, so it's a good idea to master these folds and bases before you start. When making the projects, follow the key below to find out what the lines and arrows mean.

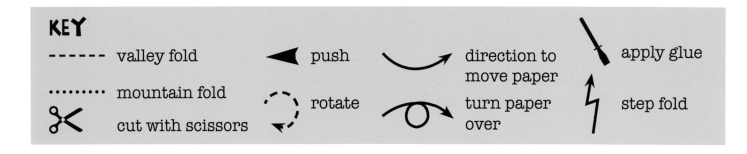

KEY

- - - - - - valley fold

········· mountain fold

✂ cut with scissors

◀ push

⟲ rotate

⌒→ direction to move paper

↺→ turn paper over

⚡ step fold

↗ apply glue

VALLEY FOLD

To make a valley fold, fold the paper toward you, so that the crease is pointing away from you, like a valley.

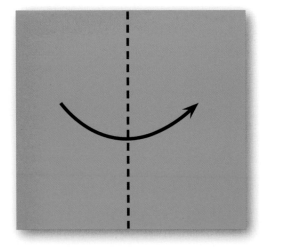

MOUNTAIN FOLD

To make a mountain fold, fold the paper so that the crease is pointing up toward you, like a mountain.

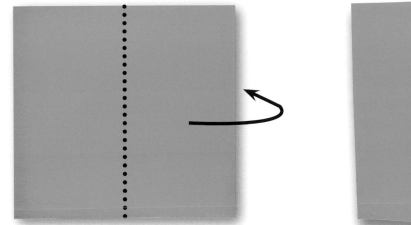

STEP FOLD

A step fold is used to make a zigzag in the paper. We'll use it to make ears, tails, and other dino features.

1 Valley fold the paper in half. Then make a mountain fold directly above the valley fold.

2 Push the mountain fold down over the valley fold and press down flat.

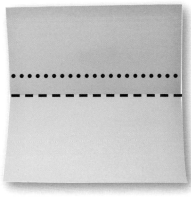

3 You now have a step fold. You can also make it in reverse, with the mountain fold first.

This is a useful fold if you want to flatten part of an origami model. It's a good way to create tails and snouts for your dinosaurs.

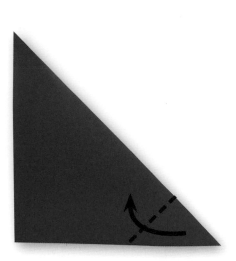

 Fold a piece of paper diagonally in half. Make a valley fold on one corner and crease.

2 It's important to make sure that the paper is creased well. Run your finger over the crease two or three times.

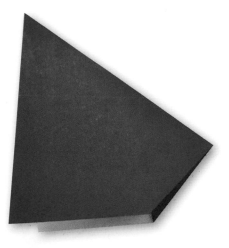

3 Refold the crease you just made into a mountain fold, then unfold. Open up the corner slightly.

4 Open up the paper a little more and then tuck the tip of the corner inside. Close the paper. This is the view from the underside of the paper.

 Flatten the paper. You now have an inside reverse fold.

OUTSIDE REVERSE FOLD

This is great if you want to make part of your model stick out. It will come in handy for making heads and crests.

1 Fold a piece of paper diagonally in half. Make a valley fold on one corner and crease.

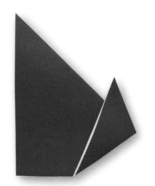

2 It's important to make sure that the paper is creased well. Run your finger over the crease two or three times.

3 Refold the crease you just made into a mountain fold, then unfold. Open up the corner slightly.

4 Open up the paper a little more and start to turn the corner inside out. Then close the paper when the fold begins to turn.

5 You now have an outside reverse fold. You can either flatten the paper or leave it rounded out.

KITE BASE

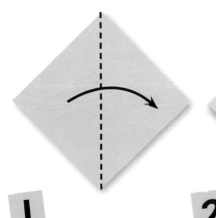

1 Place your paper like this. Valley fold it in half from left to right.

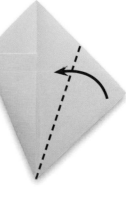

2 Valley fold the left-hand point over to the middle crease.

 Repeat step 2 on the other side.

 You now have a kite base.

FISH BASE

1 Make a kite base, as shown on page 7. Valley fold the left-hand point to the central crease.

2 Do the same on the other side.

3 The paper should now look like this.

OPEN

4 Open out the top left corner. Take hold of the inside flap and pull it down to meet the middle crease to make a new flap as shown.

OPEN

5 Flatten the paper. Then do the same on the other side.

6 You now have a fish base.

SQUARE BASE

1 Fold from top to bottom and unfold. Then fold from left to right and unfold.

TURN OVER

45°

2 Turn your paper over and rotate it so that one side is facing you.

3 Valley fold along the horizontal and vertical lines and unfold.

45°

4 Rotate the paper so a corner is facing you.

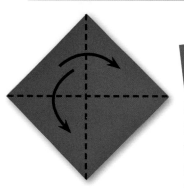
PUSH   PUSH

5 Hold the paper by opposite diagonal corners. Push the two corners together so that the shape begins to collapse.

6 Flatten the top of the paper into a square shape. You now have a square base.

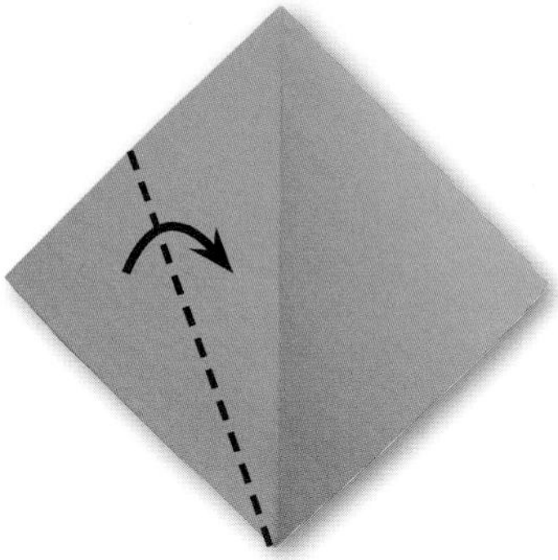

1 Start with a square base (see page 8), with the open end facing you. Fold the left-hand point of the top layer to the central crease.

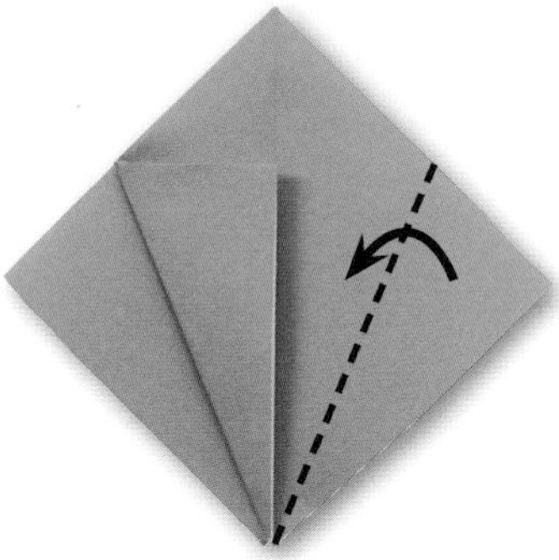

2 Do the same on the other side.

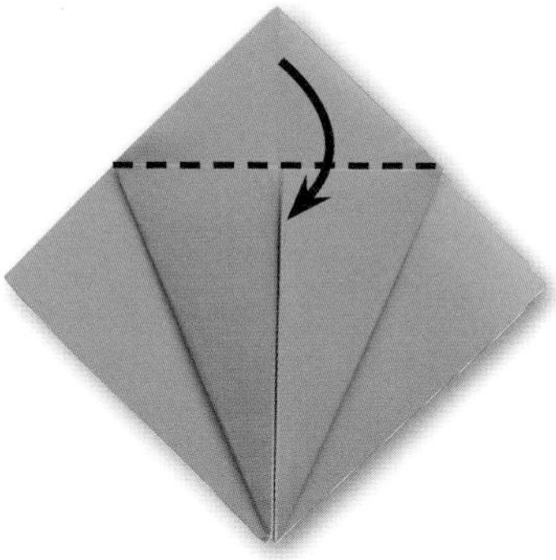

3 Valley fold the top point down.

4 Unfold the top and sides and you have the shape shown here.

5 Take the bottom corner and lift it up to the top.

6 The paper should open like a bird's beak. Open out the flap as far as it will go.

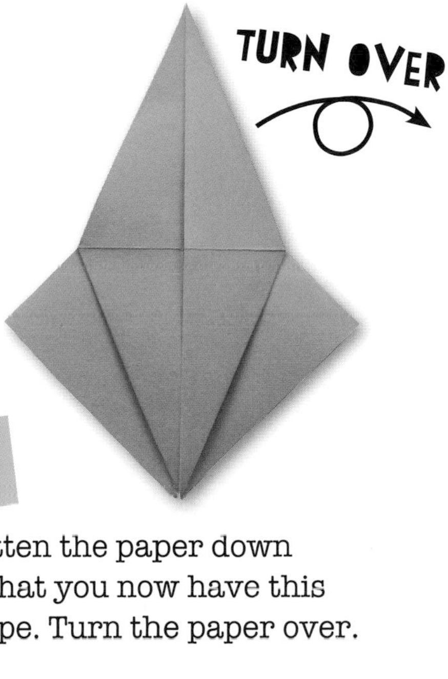

TURN OVER

7 Flatten the paper down so that you now have this shape. Turn the paper over.

8 The paper should now look like this. Repeat steps 1 to 7 on this side as well.

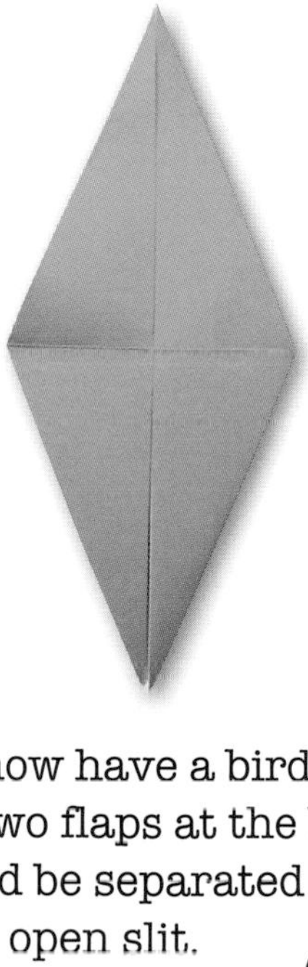

9 You now have a bird base. The two flaps at the bottom should be separated by an open slit.

9

QUETZALCOATLUS

Say "KWET-zal-koh-AT-luss"

This giant flying reptile is easier to make than it is to say. You'll need scissors to complete this project—cut carefully when you make its crest.

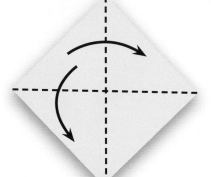

1

Place your paper like this, white side up with a corner facing you. Fold in half from left to right, and unfold. Then fold in half from top to bottom, and unfold.

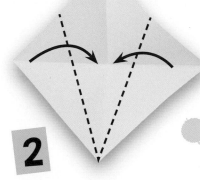

2

Fold the left and right points to the central crease, as shown.

3

Your paper should look like this. Turn it over from left to right.

TURN OVER

4

Make a large step fold, as shown (see page 5).

5

Your paper should look like this. Mountain fold it in half from right to left.

6

Now rotate your paper 90° to the right.

90°

7 Fold the left-hand point up and to the left, as shown.

★

EASY

8 Fold it the other way, so it's also a mountain fold, and then turn it into an inside reverse fold (see page 6).

q Mountain fold the top left-hand point over to the left. This is the head.

10 Fold the head down, as shown.

11 Use your scissors to make two small cuts behind the head, as shown.

12 Open up the wings of your creation.

13

Add eyes and a mouth and your flying reptile is complete.

FINISHED!

11

PLIOSAURUS

Say "PLY-oh-SAW-rus"

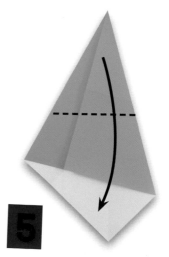

This fierce-looking creature wasn't a dinosaur—although it looked a lot like one. It was a reptile that lived in the sea. You'll need two pieces of paper for this project: one for the body and one for the legs.

BODY

1 Let's start with the Pliosaurus's body. Place your paper white side up with a corner facing you. Valley fold in half from left to right, and unfold.

2 Fold the bottom right edge over to the top left edge, as shown, then unfold.

3 Fold the right-hand point over to the crease you made in step 2.

4 Fold the top left-hand edge over so it meets up with the fold you made in step 3.

5 Fold the top point down to the bottom point.

6 Rotate the paper 90° to the right.

7 Fold the left-hand point of the upper layer back to the right, as shown.

8 Unfold all the folds you've made so far.

9 Make a small fold on the right-hand side.

10 Refold the fold you made in step 4. It's at the top of your paper now.

11 Refold the fold you made in step 3.

12 Fold the top right-hand edge over again, so it lines up with the central crease.

13 Your paper should look like this. Turn it over from top to bottom.

TURN OVER

14 Make a fold on the right-hand side, as shown.

15 Fold the right-hand side over to the left, as shown.

16 Fold the upper layer back to the right along the crease line made in step 5 to form a step fold.

17 Your paper should look like this. Put it to the side while you continue with the legs.

LEGS

1 Place your paper like this, white side up with a corner facing you. Fold in half from left to right, and unfold. Then fold in half from top to bottom, and unfold.

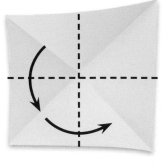

2 Turn the paper so a straight edge is facing you. Now fold in half from left to right, and unfold. Then fold in half from top to bottom, and unfold.

3 Your paper should look like this. Turn it over from left to right.

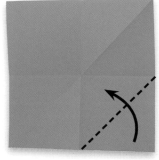

4 Fold the bottom right-hand corner up to the central point.

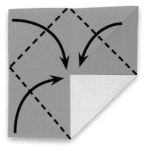

5 Repeat step 4 with the other three corners.

6 Unfold the folds you made in steps 4 and 5.

7 Turn the paper over from left to right.

8 Fold the left- and right-hand edges to the central crease.

9 Fold the top and bottom edges to the central crease.

10 Open up the paper on the top left corner. Take the central point of the second layer and bring it over to the left so it forms a triangle shape, as in the image for step 11.

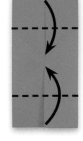

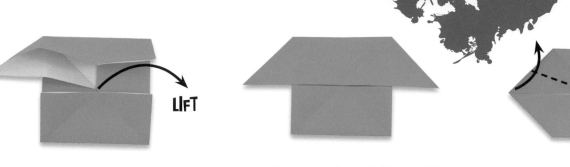

11 Your paper should look like this. Repeat step 10 on the right side.

12 Repeat steps 10 and 11 on the bottom half of the paper.

13 Fold the top left-hand point up and to the right, as shown.

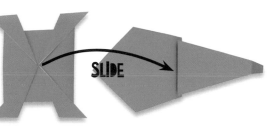

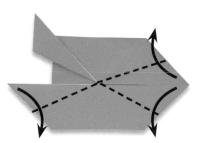

14 Repeat step 13 on the other three sides.

15 Your paper should look like this. Get the first piece of paper. It's time to put your Pliosaurus together.

16 Place your pieces of paper like this. Slide the legs over the body. Tuck the paper under the step fold made in step 16 of the body stage.

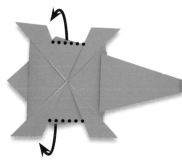

17 Mountain fold over the points at the top and bottom, as shown.

18 Start mountain folding your paper in half from top to bottom.

19 As you fold, tuck the right-hand end over to form the snout.

20

Add a fearsome set of teeth, some large eyes, and then release your new origami monster.

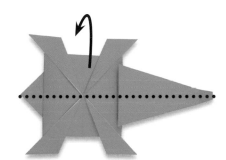

FINISHED!

ICHTHYOSAURUS

Say "ICK-thee-oh-SAW-rus"

Ichthyosaurs looked quite a lot like modern dolphins. They swam fast through the oceans looking for fish to eat.

1

Place your paper like this, white side up with a corner facing you. Valley fold in half from top to bottom, and unfold. Then valley fold in half from left to right, and unfold.

2

Fold the top corner down to the central crease.

3

Fold the bottom corner up to the central crease.

4

Your paper should look like this. Turn it over from top to bottom.

TURN OVER

5

Fold the paper in half from left to right.

6

Open up the fold on the top left-hand side, and bring the point of this flap over to the left.

7

FLATTEN

The fold you opened in step 6 should begin to form a triangle shape, like this. Flatten it down.

8 Repeat steps 6 and 7 on the bottom half.

9 Fold the right-hand point of the upper layer all the way over to the left.

10 Fold the left-hand point over to the central crease.

11 Fold the same point back again to form a step fold (see page 5).

12 Fold the paper in half from bottom to top.

13 Fold the pointed flap down to make the first fin, so it matches the image in step 14. Then repeat on the other side.

14 Fold the right-hand point up, as shown.

15 Fold it the other way, so it's also a mountain fold, then turn it into an inside reverse fold (see page 6).

16 Pull out your ichthyosaur's flippers and it's ready to swim. Be sure to give it large eyes so it can see underwater.

FINISHED!

ELASMOSAURUS

Say "ee-LAZ-moh-SAW-rus"

START WITH A FISH BASE

Although it lived in the sea, this long-necked creature had to swim to the surface to breathe. It also laid its eggs on land, much like turtles do today.

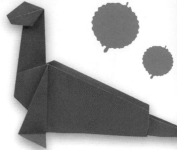

1

Start with a fish base, like this (see page 8). Rotate your paper 90° to the right.

90°

2

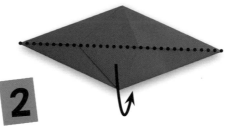

Mountain fold the paper in half from bottom to top.

3

Fold the pointed flap down and to the right to form the first fin. Repeat on the other side to make the other fin.

4

Fold the left-hand point up and to the right, as shown.

5

Fold it the other way, so it's also a mountain fold, then turn it into an inside reverse fold (see page 6).

6

Mountain fold over the left-hand point of the upper layer.

7

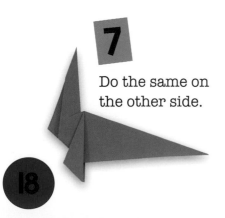

Do the same on the other side.

8

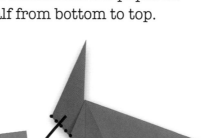

Valley fold the top point over to the left.

q

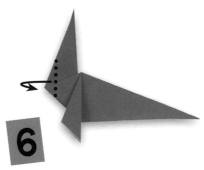

Fold it the other way so it's also a mountain fold, then turn it into an inside reverse fold (see page 6). This is the head.

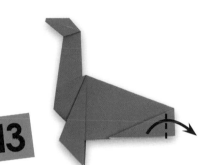

10 Fold and flatten down the upper layer of the head so it matches the image in step 11.

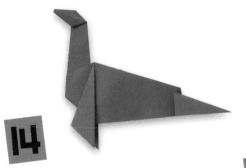

11 Mountain fold the top left point to form the snout.

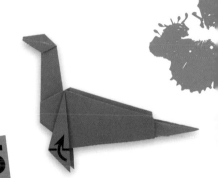

12 Fold the right-hand point back to the left. Then fold it the other way so it's also a mountain fold.

13 Make another valley fold, back to the right, as shown. Again, fold it the other way so it's also a mountain fold.

14 Turn the folds you made in steps 12 and 13 into two inside reverse folds, one inside the other.

15 Valley fold the bottom point up to create the first flipper.

16 Do the same on the other side to create the other flipper.

17 **Spread the flippers out and your Elasmosaurus should be able to stand up and waddle its way down to the shore.**

FINISHED!

SPINOSAURUS

Say "SPY-noh-SAW-rus"

This fierce predator had a large sail on its back and probably spent most of its time in water, hunting for fish and other marine creatures.

START WITH A BIRD BASE

1 Start by making a bird base (see page 9). Then valley fold the top point of the upper layer down to the bottom.

2 Mountain fold the remaining top point down to the bottom.

3 Your paper should look like this. Fold the top point down to the horizontal crease, and then unfold.

4 Fold the top point down to the crease you made in step 3.

5 Your paper should look like this. Unfold the last fold.

20

TURN OVER

6 Turn the paper over from left to right and repeat steps 4 and 5 on the other side.

7 Fold the right-hand point of the upper layer over to the left, and repeat steps 4 and 5. Then fold the point back to the right again.

★ ★ ★
HARD

8 Now, fold the left-hand point of the upper layer over to the right, and repeat steps 4 and 5 on that side, too. Then fold the point back to the left again.

9 Open out the folds at the bottom.

OPEN **OPEN**

PUSH

10 Start pushing down the top point.

PUSH

11 As you push, the creases made in steps 4 to 8 should start folding in on themselves.

PUSH **PUSH**

12 Start pushing the sides back together. When the top point is completely inside the rest of the paper, flatten down the paper.

21

13

Fold the bottom point of the upper layer up and to the right, as shown.

14

Unfold.

UNFOLD

15

Fold the bottom point of the upper layer up and to the left.

16

Start to fold the top left-hand point over to the right along the central crease, but only fold it halfway.

PUSH

17

As you fold the left point across the halfway point, start pushing the paper up so it forms a pocket.

TURN OVER

FLATTEN

18

Flatten the paper down, then turn it over from right to left.

19

Fold the bottom point of the upper layer up and to the left, then unfold.

20

Now fold the bottom point up and to the right.

21

Repeat step 16 on the opposite side by folding the top right-hand point over to the left along the central crease. Only fold it halfway.

PUSH

22

As you fold the point across the halfway point, start pushing the paper up so it forms a pocket, then flatten it down.

TURN OVER

23

Your paper should look like this. Turn it over from left to right.

PULL

24

Take the bottom left-hand point and pull it out to the left and up, so it forms an inside reverse fold (see page 6).

PULL

25

Keep pulling the paper up until it's level with the fold you made in step 22, then flatten it down.

26

Your paper should look like this. Repeat steps 24 and 25 on the other side.

27

Make a valley fold, as shown, folding the point second from the right over to the left.

28

Tuck the bottom point behind by making a small mountain fold. Repeat on the other side.

SPINOSAURUS CONTINUED...

TURN OVER

29 Take the point you folded across in step 27 and fold it down and to the right.

30 Turn your paper over from left to right and repeat steps 27 and 29 on the other side. Then turn the paper back again.

31 Make a mountain fold on the upper layer of the right-hand side, as shown. Repeat on the lower layer.

32 Your paper should look like this. Repeat step 31 on the left-hand side.

TURN OVER

33 Fold the bottom point over to the left to form the first foot.

34 Turn the paper over from left to right and repeat step 33 on the other side to form the other foot.

35 Mountain fold the upper layer on the right-hand side, as shown. Repeat on the lower layer. This is the tail.

36 Valley fold the left-hand point up and to the right.

37

Now fold the point down and to the left.

38

Pull the point to the left, then push it back to the right so that folds go out on either side of the paper, forming a step fold. This is the head.

PUSH ▶

FOLDS GO OUT ON EITHER SIDE OF THE PAPER

39

Push the tip of the left-hand point down and to the right.

PUSH ◀

40

Tuck the point inside the head to form the snout.

PUSH ◀

41

Your paper should look like this. All that's left now is to stand your Spinosaurus on its feet.

42

Give your dino big eyes to help it track down its prey.

FINISHED!

PTERANODON

Say "teh-RAH-noh-don"

Pteranodon had a distinctive crest on its head, and used its large, leathery wings to soar through the prehistoric skies. Here's how to make your own origami version.

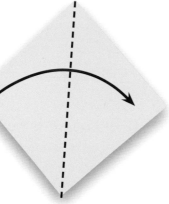

1

Fold the paper in half from left to right, then unfold.

2

Fold the paper in half from top to bottom.

3

Fold the left-hand point up and to the right to meet the central crease.

4

Repeat step 3 on the right-hand side.

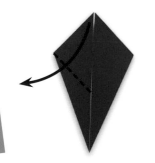

5

Your paper should look like this. Fold the top left point down and to the left, as shown.

6

Repeat step 5 on the right-hand side.

oPEN   oPEN

7

Open out the paper at the bottom and lift up the bottom point of the upper layer a little bit, so it sits in front of the other layers.

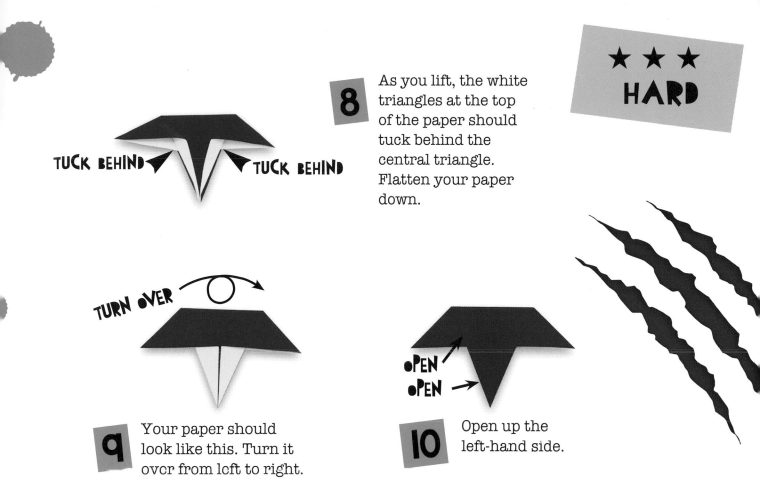

TUCK BEHIND ◄ ► TUCK BEHIND

8 As you lift, the white triangles at the top of the paper should tuck behind the central triangle. Flatten your paper down.

TURN OVER

9 Your paper should look like this. Turn it over from left to right.

OPEN
OPEN

10 Open up the left-hand side.

11 Bring the second layer of the bottom triangle out and up to the top so it becomes the first layer, and then bring it across to the right. As you do, fold the bottom left edge across to the central crease, turning the mountain fold into a valley fold.

FLATTEN
FLATTEN ►

12 Flatten the paper down.

13 Repeat steps 11 and 12 on the right-hand side.

14 Your paper should look like this (on both sides). Fold it in half from right to left.

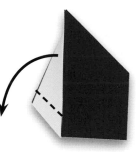

15 Rotate your paper 90° to the right.

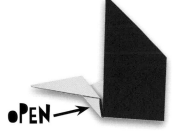

16 Fold the left-hand point up and to the right.

17 Now fold the point back down to the left, as shown.

18 Open out the folds you made in steps 16 and 17.

oPEN →

19 Fold both folds the other way, so the mountain fold is a valley fold, and the valley fold is a mountain fold. Then turn them into two inside reverse folds (see page 6), one inside the other. This is the head.

PULL

20 Pull back the top layer of the head.

21 Make a valley fold as shown.

22

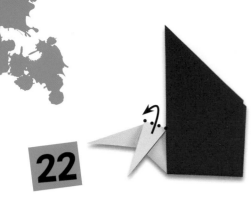

Fold it the other way so it's also a mountain fold, then turn it into an outside reverse fold (see page 7). This is the crest.

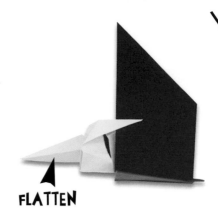

FLATTEN

23 Flatten the paper down, and tuck the head between the wings.

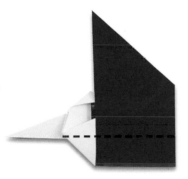

24 Fold down the top wing, as shown.

25

Now fold down the other wing, so it matches the first.

26

Your paper should look like this.

27 **Spread your Pteranodon's wings out, and it's ready to take to the skies.**

FINISHED!

GLOSSARY

crest A comb or tuft of feathers on the head of a bird or flying prehistoric creature.

dinosaur A type of prehistoric reptile.

distinctive Something that marks a person or animal apart from others.

flipper A broad, flat limb that many sea creatures use for swimming.

marine Relating to the ocean.

predator An animal that hunts and kills others for food.

prey An animal that is hunted and killed by others for food.

reptile Animals with scales or plates that breathe air, have a backbone, and lay eggs, such as turtles and snakes.

sail A broad fin on the back of an animal.

FURTHER INFORMATION

BOOKS

Harbo, Christopher. *Origami Palooza: Dragons, Turtles, Birds, and More!* North Mankato, MN: Capstone Press, 2015.

Montroll, John. *Origami Dinosaurs for Beginners.* Mineola, NY: Dover Publications, 2013.

Ono, Mari, and Hiroaki Takai. *How to Make Paper Dinosaurs: 25 Awesome Creatures to Fold in an Instant.* London, UK: CICO Books, 2018.

Schultz, Walter-Alexandre. *Origami Dinosaurs.* New York, NY: Enslow Publishing, 2018.

WEBSITES

www.origami-make.org/howto-origami-dinosaur.php
Follow the instructions on this site to learn how to fold more dinosaurs.

www.origami-resource-center.com/origami-dinosaurs.html
This website offers instructions to make over 80 origami dinosaurs!

Publisher's note to educators and parents: Our editors have carefully reviewed these websites to ensure that they are suitable for students. Many websites change frequently, however, and we cannot guarantee that a site's future contents will continue to meet our high standards of quality and educational value. Be advised that students should be closely supervised whenever they access the Internet.

INDEX